FLORENCE NIGHTINGALE

MISS FLORENCE NIGHTINGALE. L.S.Cº Nº123.

SOCIAL REFORMER AND PIONEER OF NURSING

Sarah Ridley

W

FRANKLIN WATTS
LONDON · SYDNEY

Franklin Watts
First published in Great Britain in 2020 by The Watts Publishing Group

Credits
Editor: Sarah Peutrill
Cover design: Thy Bui
Designer: Lisa Peacock

Picture credits: All images Courtesy of Florence Nightingale Museum Trust,
London except for the following: Alamy: 17t Chronicle; 38 Pictorial Press.
Getty Images: front cover br Hulton Archive, 26 Hulton Archive. LSE Library:
39. National Army Museum, London: 25t. National Portrait Gallery, London:
12. Courtesy of Florence Nightingale Foundation, London, photographer Brian
Russell, BRD Associates: 42. Wellcome Collection, London: 15t.

ISBN (HB) 978 1 4451 6863 0
ISBN (PB) 978 1 4451 6864 7

Printed in China

The website addresses (URLs) included in this book were valid at the time of
going to press. However, it is possible that contents or addresses may have
changed since the publication of this book. No responsibility for any such changes
can be accepted by either the author or the Publisher.

Franklin Watts
An imprint of
Hachette Children's Group
Part of The Watts Publishing Group
Carmelite House
50 Victoria Embankment
London EC4Y 0DZ

An Hachette UK Company
www.hachette.co.uk

www.franklinwatts.co.uk

The Author and Publisher thank the Florence Nightingale Museum, London,
for all their help with this book.

CONTENTS

"THE LADY WITH A LAMP" Illustrated London News 24 February 1855.

The **Illustrated London News** *printed this picture on 24 February 1855, alongside a story about Florence's work in Scutari Hospital during the Crimean War (1853–56). Many similar stories followed.*

THE LADY, THE LAMP AND THE LETTERS

I n 1855, Florence Nightingale suddenly became famous across Britain. People read stories in the newspapers about this brave young woman who was nursing wounded British soldiers in a military hospital far away in Turkey. Drawings of Florence carrying a lamp as she walked the wards at night added to the story. So, which bits of this famous story are true and which bits are made up?

THE LADY

Many of the stories and pictures printed in newspapers focused on Florence, one young woman from a wealthy background. In fact, in 1854, she led a team of 38 nurses to Scutari Hospital, near Constantinople (now Istanbul), with other nurses joining later. They all cared for the soldiers, working in small teams, but Florence was in charge.

However it is true that each evening, Florence walked through long hospital wards, offering words or acts of kindness to her soldier patients.

THE LAMP

The lamp Florence used was actually a lantern. Sold in the local market near the hospital, the waxed cloth sides folded down concertina-style, making it neat to store. The metal base had a holder for a candle. There are reports that a young soldier often carried the lantern for Florence, but she carried it herself as well. Many of the artists working in Britain had to guess what Florence looked like as she went about her work, which is why they showed her holding the wrong sort of lamp.

Florence carried a Turkish lantern like this one, not a brass lamp.

THE LETTERS

After her return from the Crimean War in 1856, Florence lived for another 54 years. She hated "all that ministering angel nonsense", as she called it, referring to the way newspapers showed her as a saintly nurse during the Crimean War. She devoted the rest of her life to improving people's health, using her fame to get things done.

With her cats for company, she wrote letters to get support for her work, to ask for information, to tell people about her ideas and to persuade people to make changes. She drew up tables and diagrams, and used facts to show people what was wrong and what needed to be done.

Florence's work helped to bring changes in many areas, including nursing, the health of the army in Britain and India, the lives of the poorest people in India, hospital design, workhouses and living conditions for the poorest in Britain. When she died, she left behind over fourteen thousand letters, all signed with her name:

Florence Nightingale

WHY WAS SHE CALLED FLORENCE?

On 12 May 1820, Florence Nightingale was born in the Italian city of Florence. Her parents were on a long holiday at the time, visiting Italy and other countries. Florence's sister, Parthenope, had been born the year before in Naples and was also named after her birthplace. Parthenope is the Greek name for the city.

BACK TO ENGLAND

The Nightingale family were wealthy. It was quite normal at this time for rich people to spend months, or even years, visiting places of interest. However, with two small daughters to care for, they returned to England in 1821. As their daughters grew up, the family split their time between two large homes: Lea Hurst in Derbyshire and Embley Park in Hampshire.

Lea Hurst in Derbyshire, one of the Nightingale family homes. Parthenope Nightingale drew this picture.

THE PARENTS

Florence's father, William, did not need to work as he had inherited lots of money from an uncle. He was a clever man who had studied at the University of Cambridge and was always reading books. Florence's mother, Frances, loved to have friends and family to stay, many of whom were famous writers, thinkers and politicians.

EARLY EDUCATION

Both parents were keen that their daughters get a good education. Like many wealthy families at that time, they decided to employ a governess, a young woman who lived with the family. She taught Parthenope and Florence to read and write, play the piano, sing and draw. Once they could read, she taught them French and Bible studies, showed them how to improve their sewing skills and took them on long walks. There were plenty of books in the house on all sorts of subjects, so the girls could learn about whatever took their interest.

Florence's mother gave her this writing slate to practise writing and maths. Florence wiped it clean when she needed to start again.

The sisters spent all their time together but they were turning into quite different people. While Parthenope was becoming very good at drawing and sewing, Florence was fascinated by learning and was getting ahead of her older sister in French and other subjects.

This is Florence's lunch box! It is made of wood. She probably carried her sandwiches in it when her governess took her for nature walks.

EDUCATION FIT FOR A BOY

When Florence was 11, the governess left. Rather than replace her, William Nightingale became his daughters' teacher. He thought it was important for his daughters to have a good education. This was a fairly unusual idea at the time and William was even more unusual in taking on that task himself.

A WIDE CURRICULUM

Soon William was teaching his daughters Latin, Greek, French, Italian, science, philosophy, history, geography and maths. They spent most of their time studying and it became clear that Florence was extremely clever, and also very interested in what she was learning. She worked hard at Latin and ancient Greek, translating them into English.

Parthenope drew Florence and their cousin, Marianne, sitting in one of the grand rooms at Embley Park, Hampshire. Florence is the girl reading a book and is about ten in this painting.

A SERIOUS STUDENT

Florence filled notebooks with ideas and facts that she'd read in books. She made collections of shells, coins and pressed flowers, read books about them, sorted them into different types, made lists and drew up tables to present the information. She was an excellent student and, if she'd been a boy, she could have gone to the University of Cambridge or Oxford but no universities allowed women to study at this time. Although William loved discussing ideas with his clever daughter, he had no plans for Florence to do anything with her knowledge and intelligence.

Florence collected this flower near her home in Derbyshire and pressed it, to preserve it.

Florence kept objects that interested her, such as this snake skin.

A TALENT FOR MATHS

Parthenope studied alongside her sister but was not as interested. At times, she left Florence and her father to their studies and became a great companion to her mother. She noticed how good Florence was at maths though, writing: "She has taken to mathematics … she is deep in them and working very hard."

The Nightingale family spent winters at Embley Park in Hampshire, shown here, and summers at Lea Hurst (see page 6).

GOOD WORKS, GOOD DAUGHTER

While William Nightingale was busy educating his daughters, his wife Frances was passing on different skills: how to run a large house, entertain guests and show kindness to people in the local area. She had a strong belief in Christianity and passed her faith on to her daughters.

CARING FOR OTHERS

Frances really cared about the lives of the poorer people who lived near her large homes. She often dropped off parcels of food or medicine to families in need and took her daughters along with her. At a time when most children only went to Sunday School, Frances supported a village school near the family's home in Derbyshire, paying for a teacher, books and equipment. When they were old enough, Florence and Parthenope helped out in the school.

PETS AND OTHER ANIMALS

Cats, dogs, an owl, a chameleon, a cicada, a pony and a parrot were all pets of Florence over her lifetime. She loved animals.

Out walking one day when she was 16, she came across an injured sheepdog called Cap. With the help of the local vicar, she bathed the dog's leg to reduce the swelling and wound a bandage around it, helping the leg to heal and saving the dog's life.

TAKING NOTE

Florence starting writing down which medicines were used to treat the different illnesses of the people she visited with her mother. Her notes came in useful when most of her family and the servants who looked after them fell ill with flu in January 1837. Florence spent several weeks nursing them back to health.

GOD SPEAKS

When Florence was 16, she had a strange experience. She heard God's voice:

This religious experience was to drive her forwards for the rest of her life. She was convinced that God wanted her to do something with her life and became convinced that the 'something' was nursing.

A FAMILY HOLIDAY

With his daughters turning into young women, William decided to take the family on a six-month trip to Europe. They travelled around in a horse-drawn carriage visiting beautiful places, dancing at balls, attending concerts and meeting interesting people. Florence, now 17, loved the holiday and kept a record of the different ways of life of rich and poor people in the countries they visited.

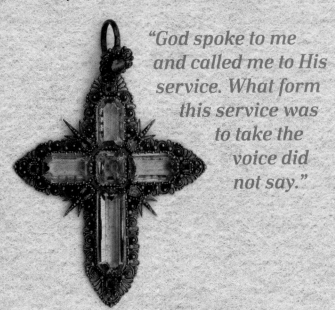

"God spoke to me and called me to His service. What form this service was to take the voice did not say."

Florence wore this crucifix as a necklace when she was growing up. She also owned many Bibles and spent long hours studying them.

Florence's cousin, Hilary Bonham-Carter, painted this picture of Florence, aged about twenty. Florence was always studying and thinking.

TO MARRY, OR NOT?

Now their daughters were in their twenties, all the Nightingale parents wanted was for them to be happily married, have children and run their own homes. Parthenope liked that idea but Florence still wanted to be allowed to train as a nurse.

ADMIRERS

Florence enjoyed dancing and met plenty of people at the parties she attended on trips to London and abroad. She was pretty and entertaining so several men were keen to marry her. One man in particular, Richard Monckton Milnes, grew very close to Florence over several years and asked her to marry him more than once. Although tempted, Florence knew she would have to give up her dreams of nursing if she married.

Richard Monckton Milnes, a poet and philosopher and the man that Florence might have married. They had lots in common and got along very well.

DREAMING OF NURSING

Throughout her twenties Florence kept asking her family to allow her to train as a nurse. Every time the subject came up, they said NO. This isn't that surprising as most nurses were uneducated, older women at this time and hospitals were seen to be dirty, dangerous places.

If wealthy people could avoid hospital they would, instead paying for a doctor to treat them at home with a servant acting as a nurse. The biggest problem for Florence was that it was not normal in Victorian Britain for wealthy young women to work as nurses, or in any other paid jobs.

FLORENCE GETS DESPERATE

Despite her family's reservations, Florence managed to visit hospitals on her trips abroad, or when she was staying with friends. She made careful notes about the buildings and how they were run. Increasingly, Florence hated her empty but comfortable life, with its endless round of parties, visitors and outings, and became restless and anxious that she would never be allowed to train as a nurse.

Worried for her health, her parents sent her on a trip to Italy in 1847–48 with some friends of theirs, the Bracebridges. Now in her late twenties, Florence loved the trip – she met interesting people, including Sidney Herbert, a British politician, and visited beautiful places. She also went to convents, where nuns nursed the sick.

ATHENA THE OWL

In 1849–50, Florence went on another holiday with the Bracebridges, visiting Egypt and Greece. While sightseeing in Athens, Florence came across some boys who were using a baby owl as a football. She rescued the tiny owl, called her Athena and brought her home. Athena became Florence's devoted companion for several years.

Florence and her pet owl, Athena, who could be quite bad-tempered. Florence is about thirty in this picture.

Pastor Fliedner, who set up the Deaconess Institute at Kaiserswerth, where Florence trained as a nurse, takes a church service attended by deaconesses.

NURSING AT LAST

In 1851, Florence's father finally changed his mind and allowed Florence to spend some time at a Christian training school for nurses and teachers at Kaiserswerth in Germany. Now their daughter was 31, William and Frances Nightingale were starting to accept that she might not get married.

KAISERSWERTH

The previous year, Florence had spent two weeks at Kaiserswerth on the way home from her trip to Egypt and Greece. Now she spent several months at the training school, where women with a strong Protestant faith learnt how to be teachers or nurses so that they could become deaconesses and help the poor. Florence watched operations take place, learnt how to care for wounds (including using leeches for bleeding patients – a cure at the time), made medicines, played with orphaned children and cared for the dying. Florence was utterly absorbed in her new life and began to feel happier. She wrote at the time:

"I find the deepest interest in everything here and am so well in body and mind. Now I know what it is to live and to love life."

Florence did not like having her photo taken. This one shows her aged about thirty in 1850.

FAMILY TROUBLES

In the autumn Florence returned home where she was loved but also felt suffocated. Parthenope was very possessive and was often upset by the idea of Florence having a life of her own. In the early 1850s, Florence's tricky relationship with her family led her to write a novel called *Cassandra* about the struggles of a young woman whose family will not allow her to do anything with her life. Although Florence often suffered from low moods, she remained determined to follow her dreams and become a nurse.

Athena the owl continued to be a companion to Florence. This is one of the pages of a book about Athena created by Parthenope.

FIRST JOB

Finally, in 1853, Florence was offered a job running a small hospital in London. The hospital cared for educated women, such as governesses, who were ill but could not afford treatment. Her family allowed her to take the job but would not let her be paid, so instead her father started to give her a yearly sum of £500 a year to live on. At work, she made many improvements to the hospital.

A year later Florence was already looking for her next challenge when a deadly cholera epidemic broke out in London, killing over five hundred people in ten days. She offered to help nurse the sick at Middlesex Hospital and fortunately did not catch the disease. Meanwhile, events far from home in the Crimea were about to change the direction of her life for ever.

WAR!

In October 1853, war broke out between Turkey (the Ottoman Empire) and Russia after Russia invaded part of Turkey's empire. The following March, Britain and France joined the war on the Turkish side.

BRITISH ARMY CAMP

Soon 30,000 British soldiers had set sail for Varna on what is now Bulgaria's Black Sea coast. They lived in tents in huge army camps, with a poor supply of food and equipment. Before long, many soldiers had caught dysentery and cholera, illnesses that spread in dirty water. Almost a thousand soldiers died without ever going into battle.

CRIMEAN WAR

Most of the fighting took place in the Crimea, now Ukraine. The main battles involved thousands of soldiers, leading to great numbers of deaths and injuries. The wounded had to survive a long journey of up to a week to reach the military hospitals as the British army had decided to place them at Scutari in Turkey, over 480 km away.

Wounded British soldiers on their way to hospital. They walked, were carried on stretchers or rode on wagons to reach boats, which brought them across the Black Sea to Scutari.

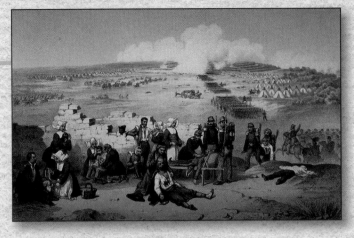

READ ALL ABOUT IT!

Soon the British people were reading newspaper reports about the awful conditions in the British army hospitals. They became enraged as they read about their brave soldiers dying in pain in filthy hospitals without enough food, blankets, medicines, bandages or nursing staff.

One reporter asked why the French army had nursing nuns, seen here at the Battle of Inkerman, while the British army only had soldier-servants called orderlies.

FLORENCE TAKES ACTION

Florence decided that she must help: she resolved to travel to Scutari Hospital with another nurse and wrote to her old friends, the Herberts, asking for their help and advice. Unknown to her, Sidney Herbert, who led the War Office, had already written to Florence asking her to take a group of nurses to Scutari to work in the military hospitals. Florence immediately agreed.

Over the next few days, Florence was frantically busy organising her trip while Parthenope and some friends helped out by interviewing women who wanted to become nurses. Many were rejected for their lack of skills or hospital experience. Half of the nurses who travelled out to Scutari were nuns with nursing experience.

Meanwhile, Athena the owl died suddenly, making Florence very sad. She wrote:

"Poor little beastie, it was odd how much I loved you."

········· = **Route of Florence and her nurses**

London → Folkestone (steam train)
Folkestone → Boulogne (boat)
Boulogne → Paris (steam train)
Paris → Lyon (steam train)
Lyon → Valence (river boat)
Valence → Marseille (steam train)
Marseille → Constantinople (Istanbul)
(paddlesteamer)

Florence left on 21 October 1854 and joined up with the other nurses two days later in France. Their long journey to Turkey, mostly by train and boat, took 13 days. It was a rough journey causing many of them to be seasick.

The Turks gave the British army the military barracks (the huge square building on the skyline) at Scutari, near Constantinople, to use as a military hospital. It was close to a cemetery.

SCUTARI HOSPITAL

Stepping off the boat at Scutari, none of the nurses could miss Scutari Hospital. Florence and her group settled into the rooms they were given at one corner of the building – and then waited for orders. Treading carefully, Florence tried not to annoy the doctors who were in charge of the hospital.

This painting shows a scene from the Battle of Inkerman, fought on 5 November 1854, with the British soldiers on the left fighting Russian soldiers on the right.

THE WORK BEGINS

At first, the nurses set to work washing floors, which were covered in a layer of poo. Even though they were short of staff, some of the army doctors did not welcome Florence or her nurses. A week later this changed when the wounded from the Battle of Inkerman started arriving at the hospital. Although the British and French side had won, thousands died in that battle: 2,500 (British), 1,700 (French) and 12,000 (Russian).

Now some of the army doctors came to Florence to discuss how the nurses could help. A group went to work in the General Hospital close by, still under the leadership of Florence, and the rest started to care for patients in Scutari Hospital, where Florence was based.

TERRIBLE STATE

Many of the soldiers arrived at Scutari in a terrible state after their journey with no one treating their wounds or illnesses. Frostbite, wounds crawling with maggots, dirty bandages, dirtier clothes full of lice, men dying of fevers – the nurses saw some terrible sights.

Soon the hospital was full to bursting. The new arrivals had to join other men lying on dirty straw mattresses or the floor. The drains were blocked, the air smelled bad, there were not enough beds, blankets, bandages, sheets or other supplies, and the kitchens were not preparing good meals. There was much work to be done. In a letter home, Florence wrote:

"These poor fellows bear pain and mutilation with unshrinking heroism, and die or are cut up without a complaint."

Parthenope drew this sketch of Florence caring for a soldier from descriptions in Florence's letters home. Florence was 34 years old by now.

WAR AND WINTER

The number of patients in the military hospitals soared after a battle but winter brought different problems for the British soldiers. Storms sank ships carrying winter supplies of food and warm clothing and destroyed their tents. Weak from the cold and eating a poor diet, soldiers fell ill in huge numbers, filling the hospitals to the limit.

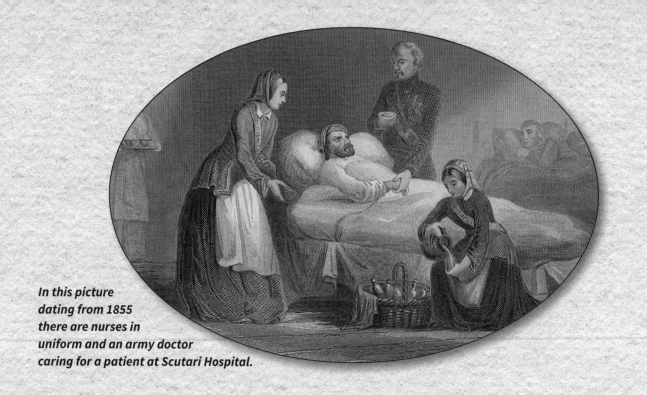

In this picture dating from 1855 there are nurses in uniform and an army doctor caring for a patient at Scutari Hospital.

THE NURSES

With Scutari Hospital filthy and overcrowded, the nurses spent a lot of their time cleaning. They washed floors and walls, blankets, sheets, bandages and the soldiers' clothes and bodies. It was a huge task.

FLORENCE AND HER RULES

Florence was in charge of the nurses. She was strict and made them follow her rules or risk being sent back to England. The nurses had to:
wear uniform,
only speak to a doctor when asked a question,
follow Florence's orders,
not get too friendly with the patients,
not go on the wards at night,
not flirt with doctors or patients,
not get drunk,
be kind to the patients.

Keeping the hospital clean was an endless task. So much of the nurses' time was spent washing and cleaning, as well as sewing shirts, making bandages, cooking and helping patients to eat their food. It was frustrating for some of the nurses as Florence only allowed the most experienced nurses to care for men with serious wounds.

THE NURSES' UNIFORM

Florence made the nurses wear the uniform they had been given by the government before they left. The women had to bring their own petticoats and underwear. Some of the nurses complained bitterly about the uniform, especially the caps, which were quite ugly. One nurse complained: " … and if I'd known, Ma'am, about the caps, great as was my desire to come out to nurse at Scutari, I wouldn't have come." The uniform included: five dresses, a cloak, a wool jacket, six aprons, six caps and a pair of rubber galoshes (boots).

To help them stand out from any other women visiting the wards, the nurses wore a sash over their apron and dress. They sewed the sashes themselves.

FLORENCE AND THE NURSES

Although she was difficult to please, Florence praised her nurses when they showed kindness to the patients. However, the awful working conditions and Florence's strict rules were too much for some of the nurses who asked to be sent home. Others were dismissed and sent home because they lacked skills or broke the rules.

When Sidney Herbert sent another group of nurses to Scutari without asking her permission, Florence felt betrayed. In a letter to Sidney Herbert she wrote:

"You have not stood by me, but I have stood by you …"

She was so cross that she nearly sent them straight home again. Florence was exhausted and saw more nurses as more work, since she would have to manage them. Once she had calmed down, she shared them out between Scutari Hospital, the General Hospital and other military hospitals nearby.

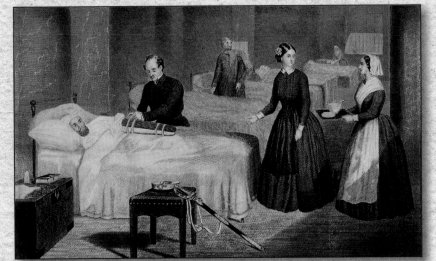

A nurse brings food for a patient, under Florence's watchful eye, while a doctor cares for a wounded soldier.

Florence and her lamp are at the centre of this picture of a ward in Scutari Hospital in 1855. The other women may be soldiers' wives as Florence banned her nurses from the wards after 8.30 p.m.

LADY WITH THE LAMP

One of Florence's rules was that she was the only nurse allowed on the wards after 8.30 p.m. Soon newspapers back in England were printing stories about 'the lady with the lamp', the nurse who walked through the hospital every evening, stopping to offer kind words or attend to the soldiers' needs.

IMPROVING THE PATIENTS' LIVES

Many of the soldiers needed amputations. These often took place on the ward. So that others could not see the operation, Florence told her nurses to put a screen around a patient who was about to undergo surgery. She watched operations when she could, to learn from them.

Now that the soldiers wore clean shirts and slept in clean beds, Florence set about improving the lives of the soldiers in different ways over the next year and a half. She set up reading rooms, wrote letters for soldiers, created a system where they could send home their wages, answered letters from families about missing soldiers and wrote letters to the families of men who had died. She even introduced a pet tortoise, called Jimmy, who was allowed to wander through the wards.

Back in England, Florence was becoming famous. Shops sold objects linked to Florence, such as this china ornament of Florence and an injured officer.

ORGANISING THE HOSPITAL

Right from the start, Florence was frustrated by the lack of equipment and supplies. As the months passed, she spent less and less time nursing and more and more time writing hospital records, notes and lists, or thinking of ways to organise the hospital better. She worked so hard that she hardly had time to eat.

She asked him to send 1,000 mops, 3,000 tin plates, 500 tin dishes, 200 pairs of scissors and 50 bottles of disinfectant (chloride of lime).

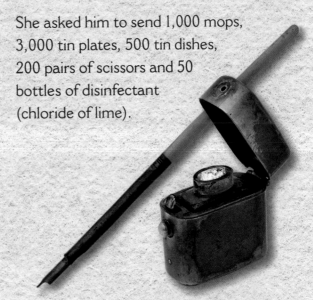

She wrote letter after letter to Sidney Herbert back in London, asking for more supplies. She used her own money as well as donations to buy what the hospital needed, and set up a laundry in the town to wash sheets and shirts. In this letter to Sidney in December 1854 she wrote:

Florence used this pen and inkwell to write letters home and to ask for more equipment.

"This morning I foraged in the purveyor's store – a cruise I make almost daily, as the only way of getting things. No mops, no plates, no wooden trays ... no slippers, no shoe-brushes, no blacking, no knives and forks, no spoons, no scissors ... – no basins, no towelling, no chloride of lime."

While most British people had begun to see Florence as a heroine, some of the army doctors found her rude and a threat to their own power. Unfortunately, Dr John Hall, the chief medical officer in the Crimea, was one of them. He wrote, "Miss Nightingale shows an ambitious struggling after power inimical [harmful] to the true interests of the medical department."

SOLDIERS STILL DYING

Sadly, despite all the efforts of Florence and her nurses, soldiers were dying in hospital in even greater numbers, mostly from illnesses. Four thousand men died in Scutari Hospital alone over the winter of 1854–55.

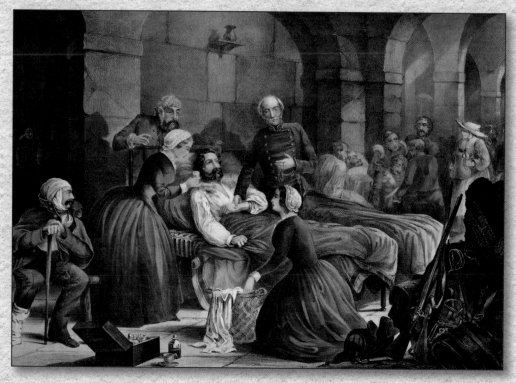

A doctor feels the pulse of a soldier while Florence offers him some medicine in a cup in this painting made in 1855.

SOMETHING NEEDS TO BE DONE

Back in Britain, the Crimean War was becoming more and more unpopular with the British people. This led to a change of government and a new prime minister called Lord Palmerston. He decided to send a Sanitary Commission to find out why so many men were dying in the military hospitals by investigating living conditions.

The Sanitary Commission reached Scutari in early March 1855. Led by two doctors and an engineer, they soon discovered that Scutari Hospital was built on top of a sewer – and it was blocked. No wonder so many soldiers were falling ill in the hospital when filthy water was seeping into tanks of water used for drinking, cooking and cleaning.

DEAD ANIMALS IN THE PIPES

Led by the Sanitary Commission, soldiers cleared a dead horse from a water pipe as well as several dead dogs from waste pipes. Now clean and dirty water flowed properly. Then they moved onto the building, replacing rotten floorboards, adding windows so that fresh air could flow through the hospital and painting walls. They left orders for orderlies to empty toilet waste daily.

Dr John Sutherland (left) and Robert Rawlinson (right) led the Sanitary Commission sent to the Crimean War in 1855. They investigated living conditions in all the military hospitals, not just Scutari Hospital.

FLORENCE'S RELIEF

That spring, far more soldiers started to recover from illnesses and return to health. Florence became friends with Dr Sutherland. She wrote in one of her letters:

"The Sanitary Commission is really doing something, & has set to work burying dead dogs & whitewashing infected walls, two prolific causes of fever."

Florence of course did not know that Scutari Hospital was built on top of a blocked sewer. No amount of cleaning could have prevented diseases from spreading until it was cleaned out. Thankfully winter was coming to an end so soldiers were no longer arriving almost dead from frostbite or illnesses caused by poor food and lack of warm clothing back in the army camps.

Florence brought this medicine chest with her, stocked with medicines to treat diseases such as dysentery and fevers. You can see it in the painting opposite.

VISITING THE FIELD HOSPITALS

By the summer of 1855, Florence felt happy enough with Scutari Hospital to plan a trip to the army hospitals closer to the battlefields. She set sail for Balaclava, across the Black Sea, with some companions.

THREE CHEERS FOR FLORENCE!

For the first time Florence saw British soldiers in the trenches near Sevastopol, a port city they had been trying to capture from the Russians since October 1854. Her fame had spread through the army and she was touched when some of them gave 'three cheers for Florence Nightingale' as she left. She also visited the vast army camp where they lived when they weren't in the front line trenches.

The British army camp stretched across hills and valleys near the port of Balaclava.
The men lived in tents, with a few wooden huts acting as hospitals or laundries

FIELD HOSPITALS

Florence and her companions visited the field hospitals and the bigger hospitals. Some of the army doctors admired Florence and took on her ideas willingly while others disliked being told what to do by a woman. Working with Alexis Soyer (see pages 28–29), she rearranged the kitchens and improved the meals for patients at the main hospital in Balaclava. Over the next few months, she was looking forward to making many more improvements.

Florence travelled about on horseback in the Crimea. In this sketch she is visiting a cemetery.

FEVER STRIKES

Only a few days later, Florence fell ill with a terrible fever. For ten days her doctor did not know whether she would live or die. This illness was probably brucellosis, caught by eating untreated goats' milk or cheese. Thankfully she survived but was so weak that she had to be carried off the boat on her return to Scutari several weeks later. Her family and friends wanted her to recover in England but she insisted on staying. She was soon back at work, before she was properly well.

THE FAMILY BACK HOME

Throughout the war Florence and her family and friends kept in touch by writing letters. Although they worried about Florence, her mother and sister were impressed by her fame. Poems and songs dedicated to Florence arrived at the Nightingale family homes, while baby girls, ships and racehorses were named after her.

The family tried to protect her privacy by not supplying family photos or letters to the newspapers. One of her fans was Queen Victoria who gave Florence a brooch designed by Prince Albert in 1855 with the words: "To Miss Florence Nightingale, as a mark of esteem and gratitude for her devotion towards the Queen's brave soldiers."

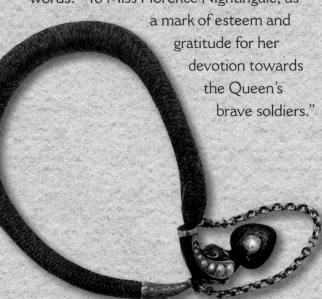
Florence wore this bracelet woven from the hair of her mother, father, sister and cousin during the war, showing her close connection to her family.

ALEXIS SOYER AND MARY SEACOLE

Florence and her nurses were not the only people trying to help British soldiers fighting in the Crimean War. There were others who made a big difference, including Alexis Soyer and Mary Seacole.

THE SOLDIERS' DIET

Alexis Soyer was a French celebrity chef who had become famous for the food he cooked in London. He funded his own trip to Scutari and met Florence to discuss how the soldiers' meals could be improved in military hospitals. He recognised that many of the men were ill because they were eating a poor diet, badly cooked. One of his trips to Balaclava was with Florence (see page 26), where he helped reorganise the kitchens and introduce new recipes, as well as providing a cooking stove that the army could move from camp to camp.

A page from Alexis Soyer's book, A Culinary Campaign. *Alexis stands beside the travelling stove he invented.*

MARY'S MISSION

Alexis met Mary Seacole when he visited the army camp at Balaclava. Like Florence, Mary decided she must go out to the Crimea to nurse injured and ill British soldiers. Her mother had taught her how to nurse and make herbal medicines when she was growing up in the British colony of Jamaica. She had already nursed British soldiers there and felt driven to help them again in the Crimea.

This drawing shows Alexis Soyer (in the doorway) meeting Mary Seacole (the only woman) in her British Hotel. It was printed in Mary Seacole's book, **Wonderful Adventures of Mrs Seacole in Many Lands,** *published in 1857.*

When Mary travelled to London in late 1854 to offer her services as a nurse, she was turned down, probably partly because she was black and also due to her age. Instead, in 1855, she used her own money to travel to the Crimea. Arriving in Scutari, she spent a day and a night at Scutari Hospital and, according to her memoir, met Florence who asked:

"What do you want, Mrs Seacole – anything that we can do for you? If it lies in my power, I shall be very happy."

THE BRITISH HOTEL

With her business partner, Mary set up the British Hotel near Balaclava. She rented rooms to poorly army officers and sold hot meals, drinks, food and useful goods. These sales helped to fund her trips into the army camps and even onto the battlefields, where she gave food and medicine to wounded men. The kindness she showed to soldiers gained her the nickname 'Mother Seacole'.

The journalist William Howard Russell wrote that Mary: "… is a warm and successful physician, who doctors and cures all manner of men with extraordinary success. She is always in attendance near the battlefield to aid the wounded, and has earned many a poor fellow's blessings." Mary Seacole stayed in the Crimea until the war ended when she returned to England, penniless.

THE WAR ENDS

The Russians put up fierce resistance but eventually agreed peace terms, bringing the Crimean War to an end in March 1856. By then, the military hospitals at Scutari were clean and well organised and the field hospitals had improved too. Gradually the British army and its nurses set off for home.

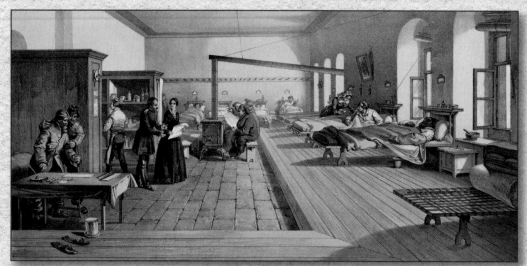

Compare this painting of a clean, tidy ward in Scutari Hospital in 1856 with those on pages 4, 20 and 22. Florence is shown here talking to a doctor by the doorway.

HOME

Florence stayed until the last nurse had left before travelling back to England under the name 'Miss Smith', to avoid any fuss. She did not welcome how famous she had become. Exhausted, she spent a few months with her family, recovering her strength, but was haunted by the death of so many men in her hospital. She wrote:

"I stand at the Altar of the murdered men and while I live I fight their cause."

That summer she was invited to talk to Queen Victoria about her experiences and she used the opportunity to ask her to support a Royal Commission on the health of the army. This work would occupy Florence for the next few years.

GIFT FOR NUMBERS

In November 1856, Florence moved to live in a London hotel where she could work and be close to government. Florence loved statistics and saw them as God's work, saying:

"To understand God's thoughts, we must study statistics, as these are the measure of His purpose."

With the help of experts in statistics, health and the army, Florence collected facts and figures, asked questions, wrote notes and published reports. What they discovered was shocking: far more of the deaths in the army hospitals during the Crimean War were from disease than from wounds, and the death rate at Scutari Hospital was higher than most of the others. In fact 16,000 of the 18,000 deaths in the Crimean hospitals were from disease.

INFOGRAPHICS

Florence did not try to cover up these facts but instead set about presenting the information in a way that was clear to everyone. As well as writing some short reports and a very long one, she worked with William Farr, a talented statistician, to create the 'Rose Diagram' (below).

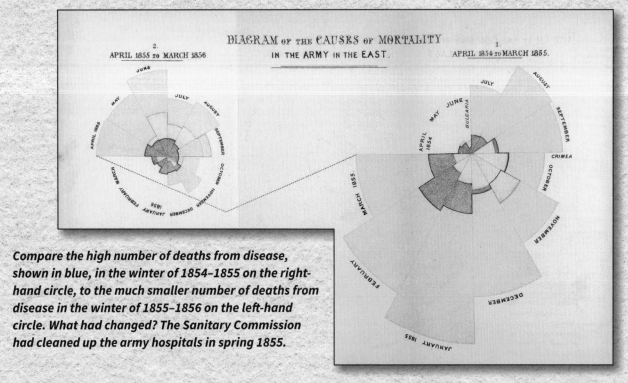

Compare the high number of deaths from disease, shown in blue, in the winter of 1854–1855 on the right-hand circle, to the much smaller number of deaths from disease in the winter of 1855–1856 on the left-hand circle. What had changed? The Sanitary Commission had cleaned up the army hospitals in spring 1855.

CONFINED TO BED

While working on the Royal Commission, Florence's Crimean illness returned. Florence spent days and days in bed with back pain, weakness, fever and depression. These symptoms returned over and over again for the next twenty years. Saving her energy for her work, she often refused to see her family or visitors, unless they were linked to her work. Servants cooked and cared for her while her cats kept her company.

NIGHTINGALE NURSES

While Florence was still at Scutari Hospital, a fund was set up to honour her work. The aim was to raise money to pay for nurses to be trained for work in hospitals.

NIGHTINGALE FUND

All sorts of people donated money and continued to do so even after the Crimean War had ended. By the late 1850s the total stood at £44,000 (worth roughly £2 million today). As time passed, people began to ask when the training school would open. Although Florence was absorbed in her investigation into why so many soldiers had died in the hospitals of the Crimea, she helped to set up the school. It opened in June 1860 and the fund also paid for a small training school for midwives.

NIGHTINGALE SCHOOL OF NURSING

The school was linked to St Thomas' Hospital in London, where the nurses would gain their work experience. Wearing brown dresses, white caps and aprons, the probationers trained for a year, learning basic nursing skills, and then had to work at the hospital for three years.

Mrs Sarah Wardroper, a matron at St Thomas' Hospital, ran the training school, leaving Florence to return to her other work.

FLORENCE TAKES ACTION

By the early 1870s, Florence realised that all was not well with the nurses' training. The probationers spent most of their time working on wards at St Thomas' Hospital but received little teaching in return. With the help of one of the doctors at the hospital, the training improved, with lectures about diseases, the human body and nursing skills.

After this, Florence remained more involved with trainee nurses as well as the 'Specials', who paid to train at the school. Florence wrote letters containing advice and support to nurses, invited some of them to tea and helped them to find good jobs. When nurses took jobs at other hospitals, they passed on their skills to others. Early on, nurses from the school went out to Australia and Canada.

Angelique Pringle was one of Florence's favourite nurses. She went to work in Edinburgh Royal Infirmary and transformed the training of nurses in the Scottish city.

NOTES ON NURSING

Florence wrote a book called *Notes on Nursing, What it is and what it is not*, published in 1860. Although she wrote it to help people care for members of the family when they fell ill at home, it was soon being used as a textbook in hospitals. Her advice ranged from the need to be quiet around a patient to the importance of being an observant nurse. She held strong views about what made a good nurse and wrote:

"The very ABC of a nurse is (A) to be sober and chaste, (B) strictly honest and true, (C) and kind and devoted."

LETTERS ... FOURTEEN THOUSAND OF THEM

On her return from the Crimean War, the people who lived near her family home in Derbyshire had given Florence a beautiful writing case as their way of thanking her for nursing soldiers during the war. It was a great gift for someone who wrote over fourteen thousand letters in her lifetime, as well as two hundred reports and several books.

LETTERS

Letter writing was a way for Florence to explain her ideas to other people, persuade them to give her their support or help, request information and record her thoughts. She got a lot of her work done by exchanging letters with people in power in government or the army. Of course, everyone wrote letters in the Victorian period (1837–1901) to keep in touch with family and friends as there were no phones or computers.

Florence's writing case. It was a place to store writing equipment including an ink bottle, pens, writing paper and envelopes. The lid folded back on itself to create a writing surface.

'THE MEMBER FOR MISS NIGHTINGALE'

In 1858, Parthenope's life changed completely, and for the better. Aged 39, she married Sir Harry Verney, a politician, and moved to Claydon House in Buckinghamshire. Parthenope worried that her marriage would take her away from Florence, but Florence was already living in London by then. Although Florence was too unwell to attend the marriage, she sent congratulations to her sister:

"God bless you, my dear Pop – and take my blessing and my best thoughts with you on your marriage day."

Florence found her new brother-in-law very useful as they shared some interests. As he was a Member of Parliament, she requested that he ask questions in the House of Commons to bring attention to important matters, such as hospitals. Other MPs noticed that he was often speaking for Florence and gave him the nickname 'the member for Miss Nightingale'.

INDIA

After Florence had finished work on one Royal Commission, she was asked to lead another, this time looking into the health of the British army in India. Without ever visiting India herself, which had recently become part of the British Empire, Florence and her team of experts set about gathering and analysing the evidence.

Florence reading her book in the garden at Embley Park in 1858.

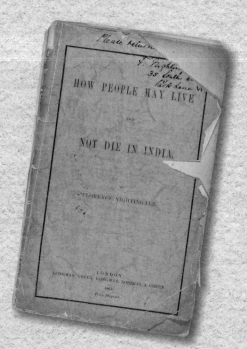

HOW PEOPLE MAY LIVE AND NOT DIE IN INDIA

Florence designed a questionnaire that was sent to two hundred army camps in India. When the team had examined the answers, they found that badly built barracks and hospitals, poor drains and a poor diet were more responsible for making soldiers ill than tropical diseases. These findings were published in the report for the Royal Commission and Florence also wrote about them in her book, *How People May Live and Not Die in India*.

A copy of Florence's book: **How People May Live and Not Die,** *published in 1863.*

For the rest of her life, Florence remained passionately interested in the health of the Indian people and became an expert. She wrote reports about how to improve life there. Horrified that millions of people continued to die of famine in India, she tried to think of solutions and campaigned for change. She was only partly successful, with the result that she became increasingly critical of the British government's actions in India.

HOSPITALS

Florence often worked on several projects at once. One project she returned to throughout her life was how to make hospitals safer. After the Crimean War, she was more aware than ever of how important the design of a hospital building can be to prevent the spread of disease.

MISS FLORENCE NIGHTINGALE.   L.S.Cº Nº 123.

Florence in 1856.

NOTES ON HOSPITALS

In 1859 some of her ideas about hospitals were published in *Notes on Hospitals*. Florence had been comparing hospitals she had visited since she was in her twenties. She thought the best hospitals had lots of windows to bring fresh air and sunlight into the buildings. One of her most important principles was that a hospital, "should do the sick no harm."

ST THOMAS' HOSPITAL

Florence advised the architects on the plans for a new St Thomas' Hospital in London. With separate pavilions or wings, connected by corridors, it followed Florence's preferred design. She liked pavilions as they divided a big hospital into several mini hospitals, helping to prevent the spread of disease. Florence was asked to advise on the plans for several other hospitals in Britain, Europe and further afield.

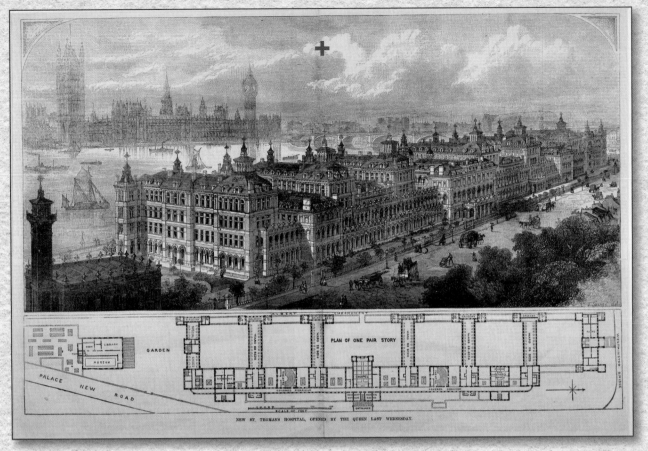

This drawing shows the newly opened St Thomas' Hospital in 1871, with its ground plan. Count the seven linked pavilions that made up the hospital.

MIASMAS V. GERMS

One of the reasons that Florence focused on the need for fresh air was that, like most people at that time, she believed that diseases were spread by miasmas, bad smelling gases in the air caused by tiny amounts of rotting material. When scientists working in the 1860s suggested that in fact invisible germs spread diseases, Florence was not alone in finding this idea hard to believe. However, in the 1870s scientists proved germs existed by running experiments and Florence gradually accepted germ theory.

As it turned out, her solution for miasmas was to clean, clean, clean. Florence wanted nurses to wash their hands often, change patients' bed sheets and bandages, wash patients using clean cloths and make sure that the wards and all areas of a hospital were properly clean. By good chance, this also stopped the spread of germs.

Named after Florence, Nightingale wards were a type of hospital ward. Windows on both sides of the long ward brought sunshine and fresh air to patients.

NURSES FOR ALL

When she was a young woman, Florence had visited workhouses, where the poorest people lived. She was shocked by what she saw, especially in the hospitals, and from the 1860s onwards, worked to improve them. She believed that, rich or poor, everyone deserved a skilled nurse if they fell ill.

Families were split up in workhouses and those who could had to work, as shown here where men are breaking stones. In return, they were given meals, clothes and shelter.

VICTORIAN WORKHOUSES

During the Victorian period, workhouses were places where people who were too poor, old or sick to be able to care for themselves, went to live. Those in charge of workhouses made sure that life was harsh, to make it unattractive to enter one. There were no proper hospitals or trained nurses in workhouses – something that Florence vowed to change.

LIVERPOOL WORKHOUSE

Florence was not the only person trying to improve conditions for people in Britain's workhouses. William Rathbone, a Liverpool merchant, was one of these people. He asked for Florence's help to introduce trained nurses into Liverpool Workhouse. He paid the wages of 13 nurses, chosen by Florence from the Nightingale School of Nursing, and they started work in 1865. From these small beginnings, medical care in workhouses slowly improved across Britain.

Henrietta Walker was one of the first trained nurses to work in the Liverpool Workhouse infirmary. After a year, she was presented with a certificate and a photo of Florence in a frame.

DISTRICT NURSES

Florence had always believed that it was best to keep people out of hospital as she thought people recovered more quickly if they were nursed at home. Again, William Rathbone had the same view and so they worked together in the 1870s to develop district nursing, where trained nurses visited people in their own homes. Rathbone used his own money to set up a training school to prepare nurses for district nursing in Liverpool. Soon other cities followed Liverpool's lead, boosted by a big donation from Queen Victoria in 1887.

FLORENCE'S HOMES

Florence never had to worry that she would end up in a workhouse through poverty or sickness. In the years after the Crimean War, she lived in hotel rooms and rented London houses until her father bought her a house in 1865. Here she lived with four or five servants to look after her and her cats for the rest of her life. Sadly there are no photos of the cats but they are often mentioned in letters, such as here, where she describes Mr Bismark, a large white cat:

"He has been made a great pet of and is the most sensitively affectionate of cats, very gentle ..."

Florence's bedroom in South Street, London in 1906 when Florence was in her eighties. We know from her letters that she allowed her cats into the bedroom.

FAMILY AND LATER LIFE

Work came before family for the first eight years after Florence returned from the Crimean War but her parents were growing old and they needed her help. She started to spend weeks at a time with them at Embley Park or Lea Hurst but still lived most of the time in London, where she continued to work on all her projects.

MOTHER AND FATHER

Florence's mother, Frances, needed servants and nurses to take care of her as she was slowly losing her memory. Despite her own illness, Florence helped her father make sure that her mother was properly cared for and also took over some of Frances's duties in the local area, visiting the sick and helping out at the school. After her father died in 1874, she took her mother to visit Parthenope and Sir Harry Verney at their home, Claydon House, and enjoyed the stay so much that she started visiting regularly.

Left to right, Parthenope (now Lady Verney), Florence and Sir Harry Verney in about 1880 in the garden of Claydon House. By this time Parthenope had developed painful arthritis.

FLORENCE'S HEALTH IMPROVES

Frances Nightingale died in 1880. Around this time Florence's own health suddenly improved. She had less pain, more energy and was able to get out and about, visiting the training school at St Thomas' Hospital for the first time. While she still used her illness to protect her from unwanted visitors or invitations, she no longer had to spend so much of her life in bed.

Parthenope and Sir Harry generously allowed Florence to invite nurses from the training school for a day out at Claydon House each year. Here Florence (sitting) and Sir Harry (standing) are surrounded by nurses in uniform in 1886.

STAYING WITH HER SISTER

Florence started to spend long periods of time at Claydon House, finding the peace allowed her to do lots of work. She also enjoyed the company of Parthenope and Sir Harry, as well as Sir Harry's children from his first marriage. She often brought her cats with her and continued to visit, even after Parthenope died in 1890.

TOWARDS THE END

All through her seventies and into her eighties, Florence carried on working. People regularly asked her advice about training nurses in Britain and elsewhere, as well as how to improve the lives of the poorest people in India and Britain. She supported fund-raising events for old soldiers who had fought in the Crimea and

wrote about the importance of people looking after their own health and wellbeing. In 1907, King Edward VII awarded her the Order of Merit, a medal to recognise her outstanding work.

In her last years, Florence's eyesight and memory started to fail and she hardly left her home in London, where she died at the age of 90 on 13 August 1910. Following her wishes, her funeral was a quiet family event at a village church near Embley Park, where her side of the family grave is marked simply:

F.N.
BORN 12 MAY 1820.
DIED 13 AUGUST 1910.

WHAT DID FLORENCE NIGHTINGALE DO FOR US?

Florence Nightingale never enjoyed the "buzz-fuzz", as she called it, around her name but yet she remains famous today. So what did Florence Nightingale do for us?

Florence was 71 when this photo was taken in one of her favourite rooms, the Blue Room, at Claydon House.

HEALTHCARE FOR ALL

Florence could not accept that poorer people in Victorian Britain had no healthcare. Her work with William Rathbone to introduce trained nurses into workhouse infirmaries gave medical care to people who could not afford to pay for it. It laid down the idea of free healthcare for all – and that would eventually lead to the creation of the National Health Service in 1948.

TRAINED NURSES

Without the Nightingale School of Nursing, Florence could not have helped to bring trained nurses into workhouses. From small beginnings, the training brought skilled nurses into hospitals in London and elsewhere. They in turn set up training schools in other cities and abroad, while others became district nurses or midwives.

Every year on 12 May (Florence's birth date and International Nurses' Day) a service is held in Westminster Abbey, London to give thanks for the work of Florence Nightingale and all nurses.

BETTER HOSPITALS

Florence's research into hospital design made her an expert. She advised people on how to build better, safer hospitals in Britain, its empire and elsewhere.

SANITATION

Florence relied on evidence to prove why things needed to change. The reports and diagrams she produced after the Crimean War sent a strong message to MPs and the army: bad drains, overcrowding and poorly designed buildings allow diseases to spread. As a result, army hospitals and barracks were improved but she also helped other campaigns to demand decent drains and sewers across Britain.

PROMOTING GOOD HEALTH

In her seventies, Florence wrote:

"What is health nursing but the cultivation of health. What is health? Health is not only to be well, but to use well every power we have."

Florence urged people to improve the surroundings of the patient – bring flowers into the room along with beautiful objects, make sure the patient could see plants out of the window, or spend time in a garden. Alongside this ran the idea that people should take care of their health in order not to become patients in the first place. Take exercise outdoors! Eat a good diet! Keep the home free of germs!

All these messages are as relevant today as they were two hundred years ago.

JOBS FOR WOMEN

Florence supported the idea of votes for women, but did not devote much time to the cause. However, she gave a huge amount of time to establishing nursing as a respectable, paid job for women and also supported people who were working for better education for women.

The votes for women campaign celebrated her achievements. This banner was carried by nurses in uniform at the National Union of Women's Suffrage Societies march through London in 1908.

TIMELINE

1820 Florence Nightingale was born on 12 May, in Florence, Italy.

1821 The Nightingale family returned to England.

1827 A governess began to teach Parthenope and Florence.

1831 William Nightingale took over the education of his daughters.

1837 Florence heard God's voice calling her to His service, which she thought was nursing.

1838 The Nightingale family went on holiday to Europe.

1842 Florence met Richard Monckton Milnes, who asked her to marry him several times.

1847 Florence went on holiday to Italy with the Bracebridges. She met Sidney and Elizabeth Herbert.

1849–50 On holiday again, this time Florence visited Egypt, Sudan, Greece and parts of Europe. Florence adopted Athena the owl and spent two weeks at Kaiserswerth Deaconess Institute in Germany.

1851 Florence spent three months at Kaiserswerth Deaconess Institute, learning how to nurse.

1853 Florence spent time at a convent in Paris, France, learning from nuns who worked in the convent hospital.
Florence was appointed Superintendent at the Establishment for Gentlewomen during Illness in Harley Street, London.

1853–56 The Crimean War. After Russia occupied land that belonged to Turkey (Ottoman Empire), war broke out between them in October. The following March, in 1854, Britain and France became involved, and Sardinia joined towards the end. Over 750,000 soldiers died in total, two-thirds of them Russian.

1854 Newspapers reported the awful conditions in the British military hospitals of the Crimea.
November: Florence and 38 nurses arrived in Turkey to nurse wounded British soldiers.
5 November: Battle of Inkerman.

1854–55 Over 4,000 men died in Scutari Hospital alone that winter.

1855 February: The *Illustrated London News* printed the famous 'Lady of the Lamp' drawing of Florence carrying a lamp as she checked on her patients. Florence became famous.
March: The Sanitary Commission arrived, sent by the British government to investigate health and hygiene in the army hospitals in Scutari and the Crimea. Following orders from the Commission, a blocked sewer and other drains were cleared under Scutari Hospital, improving hygiene in the hospital. Florence met Mary Seacole when Mary visited Scutari Hospital on her way to Balaclava, where she set up her British Hotel.
May: Florence travelled to the Crimea to visit army hospitals close to the battlefield. With Alexis Soyer, she improved the meals served to patients.
Florence fell ill and almost died. She returned to Scutari Hospital when she was well enough.
The Nightingale Fund was launched to raise money to train nurses.

1856 The Crimean War ended, with the Russians on the losing side. The British army and its nurses returned to Britain.

July: Florence travelled home using a false name, to avoid any welcoming parties.

August: Florence met Queen Victoria and gained her support for a Royal Commission into the health of the army.

1857–58 Florence started researching the causes of the high death rate in the Crimean hospitals with the help of William Farr and John Sutherland. Their work revealed that most soldiers died of diseases spread by poor hygiene and bad drains, not wounds.

1858 Parthenope married Sir Harry Verney to become Lady Verney.

Florence was made the first woman member of the Royal Statistical Society, in recognition of her great skill with statistics.

1859 Florence published *Notes on Nursing*. She started work on a Royal Commission into the state of the health of the British army in India.

1860 The Nightingale School of Nursing opened at St Thomas' Hospital, London, with its first ten student nurses paid for by the Nightingale Fund.

1861 A midwife training school opened, funded by money left over from the Nightingale Fund.

1862 Florence sent advice on how to run hospitals to the USA during the American Civil War (1861–1865).

1863 The Royal Commission into the state of sanitation in India was published.

1865 Florence moved to 10 South Street, London, her home for the rest of her life.

Florence worked with William Rathbone to introduce trained nurses to Liverpool Workhouse.

1866 Florence signed the petition presented to Parliament by John Stuart Mill asking for the right to vote to be extended to unmarried women who owned property.

1870 Louis Pasteur and Robert Koch proved the existence of microorganisms, establishing germ theory – that tiny germs (bacteria and viruses) caused many diseases.

St Thomas' Hospital reopened in a new building influenced by Florence's ideas about healthy building design. Florence improved the quality of the nurses' training.

1870s onwards Florence worked with William Rathbone to develop district nursing in Liverpool and elsewhere.

1874 William Nightingale died, leaving Florence responsible for her mother. She visited Claydon House and returned many more times in the next twenty years.

1880 Frances Nightingale died.

1880s and 1890s Florence continued to campaign for the ordinary people of India to have good drains and better lives, and for improvements in the living conditions of poorer people in Britain. She was asked for advice on how to set up training schools for nurses in other countries and advised people on the importance of maintaining their own health and wellbeing.

1890 Parthenope died.

Florence made a recording that was sold to raise funds for survivors of the Crimean War.

1896 Florence published her last paper about health in India.

1900 Florence made her last address to nursing students.

1901 Queen Victoria died and Edward VII became king.

1907 King Edward VII awarded Florence the Order of Merit for her lifetime's work.

1910 Florence died at home in London, aged 90, and was buried at East Wellow in Hampshire.

GLOSSARY

altar Usually the Christian table where communion is prepared but also in ancient times, a flat rock or table used to offer a sacrifice to God, or gods.

amputation An operation to cut off someone's arm, leg, finger or toe.

analyse To examine information (or an object) in detail in order to understand it and draw information from it.

Balaclava A port city on the Crimean Peninsular, close to Sevastopol, held by the Russian forces. The British, French and Turkish forces used it as a base during the Crimean War.

barracks A large building, or group of buildings, where soldiers live.

blacking Black shoe polish.

chaste Not having a sexual relationship with anyone but the person you are married to.

cholera A disease that is passed on in dirty water. It causes diarrhoea and vomiting, and often leads to death.

Christianity The religion that is based on the teachings of Jesus Christ.

colony A country under the control of another country.

commission An official group of people given the responsibility to investigate something, or control something, usually for the government.

concertina-style Something that has a series of folds, looking a bit like a musical instrument called a concertina or accordion.

convent A building where nuns live.

Crimean War A war fought by Britain, France and Turkey (Ottoman Empire) against the Russian Empire between 1853 and 1856. The battles took place on the Crimean Peninsular, now Ukraine.

deaconess A woman of a strong Protestant (Christian) faith who lives a life of helping the poor and the sick.

diet The food and drink usually eaten by a person or animal.

district nurse A trained nurse who visits patients in their own homes.

dysentery A serious illness that causes diarrhoea and fever, and can lead to death.

famine When a large group of people have no food to eat over a period of time, leading to starvation.

field hospital A temporary army hospital close to where fighting is taking place.

frostbite Damage to fingers, toes, ears or nose caused by cold temperatures.

governess A woman paid to teach the children of a rich family in their own home. A governess lived with the family.

herbal medicine Pills, medicine or creams made from herbs to prevent or treat illness.

Herbert, Sidney (1810–1861) A Conservative Member of Parliament and the Secretary of State for War during the Crimean War. He helped Florence Nightingale during the war and worked with her to reform the health of the army.

Jamaica An island country that is in the Caribbean Sea. It was part of the British Empire from 1707–1962.

laundry A place equipped to do a lot of washing of clothes and household linen (towels and sheets).

lecture A talk given to a group of people to teach them about something.

leech A worm that lives in water. In the past, doctors often used leeches to suck blood from sick people as a cure.

lice (louse) Sucking bugs that live on animals' bodies.

low mood Feeling unhappy, sad or depressed.

maggot The young of a fly. It looks like a short worm and feeds on rotting food or animals.

matron In a hospital, the head nurse.

midwife A nurse trained to help women during pregnancy and childbirth.

mutilation Serious damage to someone's body, especially when part of it is cut off.

nun A woman who lives in a religious community and has dedicated her life to God's service.

observant Good at noticing things.

orderly A soldier who looked after patients in British military hospitals, moving them, helping doctors, giving out medicine and other tasks. He did not have any proper medical training.

orphanage A home for children whose parents are dead, or are unable to look after them.

petticoat A thin dress or skirt worn as underwear under other clothes.

philosopher Someone who studies philosophy, the study of ideas about knowledge, morals and other big questions about human life.

physician In the past, another name for a doctor.

possessive Not wanting someone to be independent and demanding much of their attention or love.

probationer A student nurse at the Nightingale School of Nursing.

prolific Producing a great number of something, in this case, a great number of the causes of fever.

pulse The steady beat of blood as it is sent around the body by the heart. It can be felt at certain points on the body, such as the neck and wrist.

purveyor Someone in charge of supplies.

Rathbone, William (1819–1902) A Liverpool merchant who worked with Florence Nightingale to set up district nursing and improve medical care in workhouses.

reading room A place where people can read books or study.

Royal Commission A group of people who are chosen by the British government to examine a subject or law.

Royal Statistical Society The society founded in 1834 to promote the importance of statistics and data.

sanitary Keeping places clean and healthy.

servant A person who cooks and cleans for someone in their house.

sewer An underground pipe for carrying dirty waste water away from houses and buildings.

slum A house that is in a bad state of repair, usually in a poor area of a town or city.

sober Sensible, serious and not drunk on alcohol.

Special The name for nursing students at the Nightingale School of Nursing who could afford to pay for their training.

statistician Someone who works with numbers and data to draw out information from them.

suffrage The right to vote in political elections.

Sunday School During the Victorian period in Britain (1837–1901), thousands of children attended free Sunday Schools to learn about the Bible and learn to read and write at a time before the government provided schools for all in 1870.

training Learning the skills needed to do a job, such as nursing.

trench In wars, long, deep ditches dug to provide protection and shelter for soldiers on opposing sides.

tropical Coming from the hottest parts of the world, between the Tropic of Cancer and the Tropic of Capricorn.

ward A room in a hospital for people of the same age, or suffering from the same kind of illness or condition.

whitewash A type of white paint made up of chalk or lime and water, used to make buildings look clean and bright.

workhouse In the past, a building where the poorest people in society were sent to live and given work.

FURTHER INFORMATION

Florence Nightingale Museum
www.florence-nightingale.co.uk

The museum dedicated to Florence Nightingale. Search its collections to see all sorts of material relating to Florence. The website has fact sheets about Mary Seacole, Alexis Soyer and Florence Nightingale. Visit the museum on the St Thomas' Hospital site in London.

Claydon House
www.nationaltrust.org.uk/claydon

Visit Lady Parthenope Verney and Sir Harry Verney's home in Buckinghamshire, now run by the National Trust. Find out more about Florence's connection to the house, where you can also see her bed!

University of Nottingham, Florence Nightingale Comes Home for 2020
www.florencenightingale.org/florence-nightingale-in-derbyshire/nightingales-connections-to-derbyshire.aspx

University of Nottingham project linked to the bicentennial of Florence's birth. Includes information about her links to Derbyshire.

National Army Museum
www.nam.ac.uk/subjects/crimean-war
Learn more about the Crimean War on their website and visit the museum in London.
www.nam.ac.uk/explore/florence-nightingale-lady-lamp
This area of their website is all about Florence Nightingale and the Crimean War.

Science Museum, London
www.sciencemuseum.org.uk/objects-and-stories/florence-nightingale-pioneer-statistician

Objects, paintings and photos highlight Florence Nightingale's scientific and mathematical approach to problems.

National Archives, London
www.nationalarchives.gov.uk/education/resources/florence-nightingale

A lesson plan on Florence Nightingale suitable for KS1 and KS2.

International Nurses' Day
www.icn.ch/what-we-do/campaigns/international-nurses-day

BBC
iWonder guide: Florence Nightingale: Saving lives with statistics
www.bbc.com/timelines/z92hsbk
Mark Bostridge, acclaimed biographer of Florence Nightingale, worked on this guide.

www.bbc.com/teach/class-clips-video/history-ks1-ks2-florence-nightingale/z68fcqt
BBC Teach film about Florence Nightingale.

www.bbc.com/ideas/videos/what-would-florence-nightingale-make-of-big-data/p075lxkt
BBC film about Florence Nightingale and her love of statistics.

INDEX